Personality Development Guidelines

Author Suffian Ansari

Table of Content

Personality Development

Personality is the combination of thoughts, behaviours, feelings that form an individual distinctive character.

To be successful in life we must groom our personality and look good in front of others. But how we can develop and groom our personality and look different among the people? First understand, why do we need to groom our personality.

Because we don't want to be like a person who:

- looks lazy
- always unpunctual
- dejected
- lacks self confidence
- unable to make decisions
- don't socialize with people

To groom our personality, we must understand about communication process, negotiation skills, time management, stress management.

Communication Process

Communication is an exchange of information from one person to other person or a group of people.

Why do we need to understand communication process to improve our personality? Because if we cannot communicate and listen in the best manner, we cannot explain and understand a basic statement.

Communication process

Communication process consists of following

Communicator: who sends the message

Medium: through what source message is transmitted, example face to face, email, social media, letter

Receiver: who receives the message

Noise: anything that can distort the message

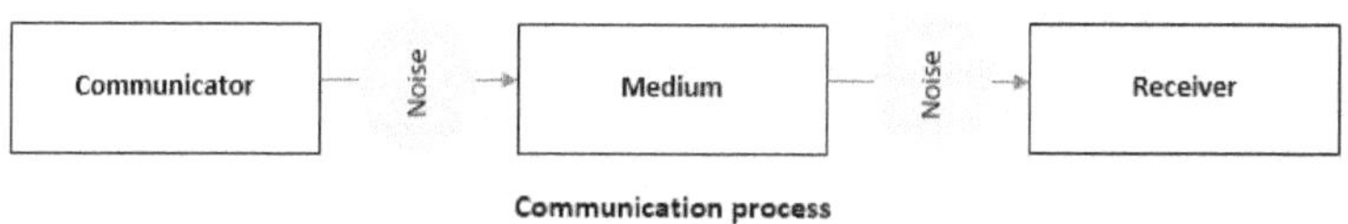

Communication process

Communicator sends the message through a medium and then the message is received by the receiver. Noise can disturb the message. If you are talking on the phone and an aeroplane passes nearby you with a lot of sound and your receiver cannot hear the caller voice except aeroplane sound, this aeroplane sound is considered as noise.

There are different types of communication, verbal and nonverbal.

Verbal communication

This communication involves sharing of information using words. Verbal communication consists of oral and written communication. This communication can be face to face, group discussions, live video conferencing, letters, memos, emails.

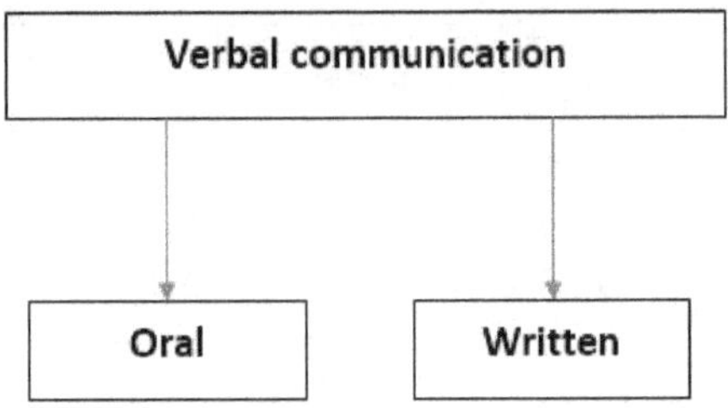

Oral communication

This communication involves expressing information and words by mouth. Face to face oral discussion between two people is an example of oral communication.

Written communication

This involves expressing information and words in written form. Drafting and sending email to a customer is an example of written communication.

Non-verbal communication

When messages or information is exchanged or communicated without using any spoken or written word is known as nonverbal communication. Non-verbal communication takes place through gestures, facial expressions, eye contact, physical proximity, touching.

- Gestures are movement of our body parts for expressing information
- Posture is how we position our body, like how we sit, stand etc.
- Body language is a behaviour to express information. It includes combination of gestures, postures, eye contact, facial expressions like smiley or angry face. Through body language another person can assume that a person is angry or happy

Formal and informal communication

Formal communication

Formal communication is the communication which occurs through predetermined channels. Communication between 2 departments through email, memo, letter are examples of formal communication. This type of communication is done in written format to have documentary evidence. Sometimes formal communication can be slow because it follows formal channels and rules. Slang words are not used in this communication. Any official communication in the organization is formal communication. Business letters, memos, contracts, agreements are examples of formal communication.

Informal communication

Informal communication has no rules and is free flow of communication. Discussing sports news with office colleagues and team members are examples of informal communication in the office. Informal communication is part of life and speed of this communication is fast. Watsapp, facebook chat with friends are all informal communication.

Negotiation Skills

Negotiation is a process in which two or more parties settle differences and reach an agreement.

Good negotiators are intelligent, and they know what point they have to say at what time. They can manage conflicts and disputes in a way so that both parties can agree mutual agreement.

To groom personality, we should understand about styles of negotiation and negotiation process.

Negotiation styles

Competing

This type of negotiation follows the principle of "I win, you lose." These types of negotiators tend to do whatever it takes to reach their desired agreement at any cost. They are result oriented and focuses on achieving short-term goals quickly. Their motive is to win, they do not consider about other party which may disturb their relationship with the party. The problem with this style of negotiation is that one wins and other loses.

Collaborative

This style follows the principle of "win-win situation". Both parties reach an agreement which is acceptable for both. This approach benefit is that relationship of the parties remains intact because of mutual agreement. And during discussion both parties can understand each other problems. People who focus on maintaining relationship, tends to focus on collaborative negotiation.

Compromise

This style follows the principle of “I win/lose some, you win/lose some” and it is different from collaborative because it is not a win-win situation for both parties. When reaching the terms of the agreement both parties must make compromises to conclude the agreement.

Accommodate

This style follows the principle of “I lose, you win”. These types of negotiators are opposite of competitive negotiators. They focus on preserving relationships and building a friendly rapport by sacrificing some of their company’s interests in favour of the opposite party’s interests.

Avoid

This style follows the principle of "I lose, you lose". These negotiators hate conflict and tend to talk in ambiguous terms about the issue and do not like to reach agreement. The main goal of these negotiators is to avoid reaching any agreement. These styles work best in situations where the negotiation concerns a matter, that is unimportant to both parties.

Negotiation process

Negotiation process consists of following steps

- Preparation
- Introduction
- Exchange of information and facts
- Bargaining
- Agreement

Preparation

Well prepared negotiator may win the negotiation. To get well prepared, get the maximum information, history, strengths, and weaknesses of other party, prepare your agenda on which negotiation will be conducted, and make your BATNA – best alternative to a negotiated agreement. BATNA are the alternatives, if in case negotiation fails, negotiator can offer other alternative proposals to reach an agreement. Negotiator should also gather information about the culture and norms of other party, example other party may like to come in the meeting with local dress. These factors can make impact on the negotiation.

Introduction

On negotiation day, negotiator should be on time to arrange himself/herself and the documents, start the negotiation by introducing himself/herself, the team and exchange greeting. It is always good to show positive body language to boost self-confidence.

Exchange of information and facts

During this stage information exchange occurs and every party explains their case. Both parties should be able to understand each other case and ask questions to clarify things. Presentation of the case should be precise and clear so that less time can be wasted on asking too many questions and other party can understand the case.

Bargaining

Both parties should discuss how they can mutually reach an agreement which is beneficial for both, evaluate each other case and decide what they can offer. But sometimes this is not the case. Other party may not compromise on the agreement. This depends on case to case, and negotiators can offer alternative proposal to reach an agreement. Negotiation may go for agreement phase or talks may go for hold and continue again after some time.

Agreement

This is the final stage of the process in which agreement takes place. Verbal agreement may occur at the end of the negotiation and written documentation may be completed later. In most parts of the world agreement is a written and legal document.

A good negotiator should possess following qualities

- Ability to adjust styles of negotiation according to the situation
- Ability to ask questions at the right moment and offer proposal by linking other party needs
- Ability to negotiate with facts and figures rather than vague statements
- Ability to develop relationship with other party
- Ability to influence other party to reach an agreement
- Ability to control emotions, develop trust with other party and maintain ethics
- Must have good communication and listening skills
- Must possess skills to understand other party culture

A good communicator should know how to negotiate which improves in grooming personality. A good communicator and negotiator build a good reputation among communicators and audience.

Time Management

Time management is very important in life. Without time management we cannot progress in personal and professional life.

Here are some techniques which we can use to better manage time:

Plan and organize your work

The first thing you must do is to write down your task in your personal diary or you may note down your task in a software, app, to do list. By noting the task, one can plan and organize without wasting time, a person can view daily, weekly, monthly tasks and prioritize them.

Set a time limit for each task

Set a time limit for every task you perform. This time limit will allow you to organize your work for each task. Example if you have 2 meetings of 30 minutes each. You can plan your meeting points, which can be compiled in 30 minutes. If you are working in an office you can plan, in how much time I must complete each task, so that you can finish your work daily.

Prioritization of tasks

Completing important tasks first is the best way to manage work. Example if you must submit a report after 1 day, and other report after 3 days, the best way to manage work is to first complete the report which you must submit after 1 day. First completing the report which you must submit after 3 days is not a good idea, you may run out of time to complete the report which you have to submit after 1 day. Prioritize the work according to deadline.

Schedule your personal work

Do time management for yourself. Just like noting down your work, also note down your personal issues, example to take medicine at a certain time, prayers time, short breaks after each work. Scheduling our personal issues will help us maintaining health and personal life.

Set reminders

Set reminders in your smartphone or laptop calendar, this will help you in focusing on work and when you are above your time limit, reminder will help you to do other tasks.

Eliminate distractions

No one likes any kind of distraction during work, but some things are out of control like your boss wants you in meeting, you get a supplier call, management wants some urgent report. But there are few distractions which we can minimize, like using mobile phone during office hours and wasting time on social media, unnecessary calls, we can reduce them by not using social media during office hours and make the phone on silent mood and attend only important calls. Eliminate your distraction the best possible way you can and focus on your work.

Track your time and tasks

Track your time and tasks completed. Evaluate are you completing your tasks on time, or you are lacking behind the time. Ask yourself why you are lacking behind the tasks, are distractions lacking you behind or you are lacking competencies to complete the work. If everything is fine, revise your time limit for each task.

Delegate task

Delegate lesser important tasks to your junior team member and focus on the most important tasks. This can be only possible if you are a manager, or you have team members who can work like this.

Clean and organize your office desk

Do not make your office desk look messy. Organize every item on your office desk so that everything can be accessed easily. This way you can focus on your work, and it will help you reduce wasting time on unnecessary things.

Take help from management tools

You can take help from a personal diary, table planner, to do list, apps, software, there are a lot of items in the market which can be used as tools.

Benefits of time management

- When your tasks are completed on time, you are a productive person
- It makes you deadline-oriented person, in professional office culture, if you cannot manage your work on time, you might lose your job because other staff might suffer due to delay in your work
- You can balance your professional and personal life with better time management
- You will be considered a punctual person not just in office, but in society also
- Better time management makes you feel stress free because you manage your time and work efficiently
- Free time can be planned and used for other productive work
- Better time management skills boost self confidence

Stress Management

Every person face challenges in life. Some challenges make our life stressful. Financial issues, workplace challenges, family matters can make our life stressful. Just like we do time management in life, we also need to do stress management in life to overcome challenges.

Identify what factors or situation makes you stressful

To manage stress in your life, first identify what factors or situation makes you stressful. If you cannot figure out what makes your life stressful, it will be difficult to manage stress and can lead to serious health consequences.

Example, you have long working office hours, you are not able to fulfil family financial obligations, or any other situation makes you stressful.

How to overcome or reduce stress

- Avoidable situation
- unavoidable situation

Avoidable situation

These are factors which can be easily ignored to avoid stressful situations. Example if you get heavy traffic on road during your office working hours and which makes you late for the office and same thing happens when you go back to home, and you become stressful due to this situation. You can reduce stress due to traffic, by altering office route, changing the time when you arrive and leave the office.

Unavoidable situation

These factors are hard to avoid and are difficult to overcome. Example you have large amount of financial loans, and you are not able to pay loan instalments on time. This will not just increase the stress level, but this type of stress can seriously affect health. In other way, if a person cannot avoid the situation, then he or she should accept the reality and focus on the solution which can reduce the stress. In the above-mentioned example, stress may be reduced when one can easily pay monthly instalment or adjust the full loan.

You must decide yourself, which situations are avoidable, and which are unavoidable for you.

Positive and negative ways to manage stress

Negative ways

Negative ways are things which are not good for a person.

- smoking
- drinking alcohol
- taking drugs for relaxation
- eating too much

- sleeping for long hours

These are some ways which can reduce stress for some period but in the long run can destroy health.

Positive ways

This is the best way to reduce stress.

- socializing with friends
- spending time with family
- walk in the park
- exploring nature
- listening to favourite music
- listening to favourite religious personality
- enjoy limited coffee or tea

These are some good ways which can reduce stress and in the long run also benefits health.

Other qualities

A person should have following qualities to better manage stress in life

- increase patience level to better focus things
- plan your personal financial issues
- keep balance between work life and family life
- adopt healthy habits
- maintain emotional balance in life
- manage your personal and workplace time

Useful guidelines to develop personality

Evaluate yourself “who are you”

Evaluate the direction of your life. It is moving in the right direction or not. Judge what you want to be, and currently what you are right now. How people consider you as a friend, colleague, relative, brother/sister, manager.

Note your goals

Always note down your goals and daily tasks you want to perform. It keeps track of daily goals and tasks, and you will not forget tasks which you want to perform.

Mentorship

Choose your mentor who can guide you in multiple aspects of life. They help to develop skills, career goals, and other prospects of life.

Improve decision making

A person with good decision-making skills is regarded by people. He or she is considered as a self-confident person.

Independent decision making improves to develop good personality.

Keep yourself neat and tidy

These are one of the most important factors in improving your personality. When a person is neat and tidy, in home or in office, it develops a good image among people with whom he or she interacts. As a universal fact, people like to interact with people who are neat and tidy and avoid untidy people. In some organizations, neat and tidy people get extra performance appraisal points. A person feels satisfied when he or she is neat and tidy and can easily communicate with people.

Increase patience and reduce anger

Anger can destroy personal and professional relationships. To be a better personality one should be able to tolerate things and able to control anger. Top leadership positions demand patience and able to control anger, not just for meetings only, but to make logical decisions in stressful conditions. In personal and professional life, patience is key to success. Low patience and frequent anger can affect people's relationship with others. If you want to develop personality, have patience, and reduce anger.

Be positive and explore new things

Keep negative thoughts away from you. Always remain positive and hopeful. Explore new things in life. Stay with people who are positive and full of life. When a person has positive thoughts and share positive thoughts with people, they admire them for sharing positive things. This builds good rapport among people, and they can assume that person has positive thinking.

Improve communication and listening skills

Communication skills is the key to success. Good communicators can influence people. If you have the skills to listen and respond appropriately, you can win hearts of people. While communicating, always be polite, maintain eye contact with audience, and maintain positive body language.

Increase your socializing

When a person meets new people frequently, that person is increasing social skills and learn new things and ideas. If you have socializing skills, it will boost your confidence. Meeting new people in the correct manner sends positive image to the people.

Identify your strengths and weaknesses

Every person has strengths and weaknesses. Identify your strengths and weaknesses and work to improve your weaknesses. Anything can be a strength, habit of helping people or work as a good team player. If you are weak in communications skills, improve your communication skills to boost your confidence.

Make your social circle with professionals

Often, we learn and behave the same way, with the people we are associated with. When we are associated with professionals, our thinking and behaviour also become like professionals. When we think and act likes professionals, these traits become part of our personality.

Learn to say "no"

Decide yourself what you can do for others and what you cannot. In professional life, if you are performing other people work, you should have confidence to say "no" with respect. If you cannot say "no" then you are sacrificing things in life.

Define a limit to do things, and how much extra you can do things for others.

Maintain emotional balance in life

We are emotionally attached with many things in life, career, family, university degree, pets. Being emotionally attached to things is not bad but being aggressively attached to things can be dangerous for ourselves. Some students feel depressed if they are unable to achieve good grades, which sometimes can lead to serious health issues. We should be able to balance our emotions, for our better health. Example if a student is unable to secure good grades, he or she must realize that this is not the end of life, one should move on and realize that he or she can secure good grades in next class, course, degree. If a person is unable to balance emotions, he or she can go to depressive mood or may lead to anger. To develop a pleasant personality, emotional balance is very important.

Record and evaluate your performance

Evaluate your goals, from where you started, and what is your progress to develop a pleasant personality.

Many tools are discussed above which guides to develop a pleasant personality. In depends on you, to overcome your strengths and weaknesses.

www.ingramcontent.com/pod-product-compliance
Lightning Source LLC
LaVergne TN
LVHW020541160826
845677LV00015B/4155

* 9 7 9 8 8 4 6 5 0 9 9 8 6 *